LITTLE TURTLE

10-4-86

BABE!

THE SPORTS CAREER OF GEORGE RUTH

BY:

JAMES & LYNN HAHN

EDITED BY:

DR. HOWARD SCHROEDER

Professor in Reading and Language Arts
Dept. of Elementary Education
Mankato State University

CRESTWOOD HOUSE

Mankato, Minnesota

CIP

LIBRARY OF CONGRESS CATALOGING IN PUBLICATION DATA
Hahn, James.
  Babe! The sports career of George Ruth.

  (Sport legends)
  SUMMARY: A biography of Babe Ruth, considered to be one of the best,
and best-liked, baseball players ever.
  1. Ruth, Babe, 1895-1948 — Juvenile literature. 2. Baseball players —
United States — Biography. [1. Ruth, Babe, 1895-1948. 2. Baseball players] I.
Hahn, Lynn. II. Schroeder, Howard. III. Title. IV. Series.
GV865.R8H33   796.357'092'4   [B]   [92]   81-5377
ISBN 0-89686-129-5 (lib. bdg.)   AACR2
ISBN 0-89686-144-9 (pbk.)

        INTERNATIONAL STANDARD   **LIBRARY OF CONGRESS**
            BOOK NUMBERS: **CATALOG CARD NUMBER:**
        0-89686-129-5 Library Bound   81-5377
        0-89686-144-9 Paperback   AACR2

PHOTO CREDITS:

Cover: Focus On Sports, Inc.

UPI: 3, 5, 6, 9, 12, 21, 22, 34-35, 46-47
Wide World Photos: 24-25, 27, 31, 32, 36, 38-39, 40,
        45
FPG: 19, 28
The Bettman Archives: 15

CRESTWOOD HOUSE

Crestwood House, Inc., Box 3427, Hwy. 66 So., Mankato, MN 56001

BABE!

CHAPTER 1

It's been more than thirty years since the death of one of the best baseball players ever.

Yet, Babe Ruth still holds five major league records. No one has scored more runs in one season than Babe's 177 in 1921. The Babe's twelve years as the league's leading home run slugger still stands.

Pitchers were so afraid to pitch to Babe, they walked him 170 times in 1923, and 2,056 times during his career. Babe still holds the record for the highest slugging percentage (.690).

In the 1920's and 30's, Babe held or shared sixty-one records. Twenty-eight were World Series records!

It surprises many fans to learn Babe was also one of baseball's best pitchers. After Babe retired, he said, "I'm proud I hit sixty home runs in one year. But I'm even more proud of pitching twenty-nine scoreless innings in the World Series."

Baseball records are only one part of the Babe Ruth legend. Many fans, players, and writers say Babe made baseball fun. Few fans paid to see games before Babe began playing ball. After he started hitting home runs, millions of people came to watch.

Babe had a wink, grin, and bow for every fan.

Babe watches another home run go out of the park.

Fans reading about Babe's youth wonder how he ended up in baseball instead of jail.

Babe was born George Herman Ruth on February 6, 1895 in a bedroom in his grandparent's house. Babe's mother's name was Katherine and his father's was George.

Babe's father owned a bar. "I hardly knew my parents," Babe said. "They worked twenty hours a day in that bar."

The bar wasn't a success for the Ruths. "We were very poor," Babe said. "There were times when we never knew where the next meal was coming from. But, I never minded. I was no worse off than most other children with whom I played."

As a young boy, Babe didn't have a ball, bat, or park in which to play baseball. "I spent most of the first seven years of my life living upstairs over the bar. When I wasn't living over it, I was living in it. In

This photo taken in 1916 or 1917, shows Babe (left) and his father in the bar that the Ruths owned in Baltimore.

the bar, I learned how to talk tough like the bums."

Babe also learned some bad habits in the bar. "By the time I was seven," Babe said, "I was chewing tobacco and drinking beer and whiskey. I didn't really like doing those things, they just seemed to be the things to do."

Babe had a rough start learning how to live properly. When he wasn't in the bar, he played in and around the Baltimore & Ohio train yards. "It was a dirty, tough neighborhood," Babe remembered.

"It took me a long time to get straightened out," Babe said. "I was a bad kid. I say that without pride. I hope young people don't make the mistakes I did as a boy. I hope they see how I was able to change my ways and do something worthwhile."

When he was young, Babe didn't know the difference between right and wrong. "If my parents had something I wanted," Babe said, "I stole it." He also threw apples and eggs at trucks, and said, "I learned to fear and hate the coppers."

As a boy, Babe didn't receive much love and care. "My mother hated me." Babe said. "Sometimes she whipped me for no reason."

Babe spent more time out of school than in. He didn't learn to read and write until many years later.

One night when Babe was playing in the bar, a fight started. Someone fired a gun at someone else.

"There's a young boy living there," a neighbor

told police when they came. "It's no place for him."

The police took Babe to court, where the judge said he was a "hopeless delinquent." The judge decided Babe had to go to reform school.

On June 13, 1902, Babe's father took him to Saint Mary's School for Boys in Baltimore. Babe was afraid, and just before his father left, he started crying. Instead of comforting his son, Babe's father just left.

A religious group of men, called brothers, taught at St. Mary's. The brothers were very strict and Babe learned to behave. Once, during a weekend, Babe was allowed to go home for a visit. The Ruths sent him back after he stole from their bar.

A few weeks later, Babe's mother became very ill. She thought she was going to die, so she asked to see her son. At home, Babe behaved badly again, so his father beat him with a whip and sent him back to St. Mary's.

Life wasn't easy for Babe at St. Mary's. He had to get up every morning at six o'clock. Before breakfast, Babe went to mass. After breakfast, Babe made his bed and went to school.

Although the brothers tried to teach Babe to act properly, he still misbehaved. "Babe was full of mischief," Brother Herman said. "There was nothing timid about him. He was always wrestling with the other boys."

This is the baseball field at St. Mary's where Babe learned to play the game.

One day during the middle of winter, a brother saw Babe sitting outside. Babe wasn't wearing a coat, hat, or gloves, just a thin shirt.

"Aren't you afraid you'll catch cold?" the brother asked.

"Naw, not me," Babe said, "I'm too tough!"

However, Babe's feelings could be hurt easily. Once, when friends asked him why his parents never visited him, he cried. "Guess I'm too big and ugly for anyone to come see me," he said.

CHAPTER 2

At age fourteen, Babe began training for a career. The brothers taught him to be a tailor. For three hours a day, Babe made blue and gray cotton shirts. "I worked on a machine that stitched the parts together," Babe said. "It wasn't easy getting those collars on the shirts correctly. But I was the best shirtmaker in the school."

Baseball helped Babe behave and mature. "Once I started playing the game," Babe said, "I was satisfied and happy. All I wanted to do was play baseball."

Catcher was the first position Babe played. He was left-handed, and at that time, left-handed catchers were not common. "I used a right-handed catcher's mitt on my left hand," Babe said. "After I caught the ball from the pitcher, I took off the glove and threw the ball back to him left-handed. When I had to throw to a base, I'd toss the glove away, grab the ball with my left hand and heave it with all I had."

A brother named Matthias taught Babe how to be a better ball player and human being. "If I hadn't met Brother Matthias," Babe said, "I may have ended up in jail."

Every afternoon after school and work, Brother Matthias played baseball with Babe and the other boys of St. Mary's. "I worked hard every day to learn the game," Babe said. Brother Matthias spent a lot of time working with just Babe. "He'd hit balls to me hour after hour," Babe said. "He corrected the mistakes I made with my hands and feet." Years later, Babe said, "Brother Matthias was the greatest man I ever knew."

During one game, Babe got into trouble with Brother Matthias. The boy pitching for St. Mary's wasn't throwing well, so Babe laughed at him.

"What are you laughing at?" Brother Matthias asked.

"They're getting too many hits off our pitcher," Babe said.

"All right, you pitch," Brother Matthias told Babe.

Babe stopped laughing and frowned. "I never pitched in my life. I can't pitch!"

"You must know a lot about pitching," Brother Matthias said. "You know enough to make fun of our pitcher. So, go ahead and show us how."

Babe surprised both himself and Brother Matthias that afternoon. He didn't let the other team get any hits for the rest of the game. Later, Babe said, "Pitching was the most natural thing in the world for me. I even threw a couple of curves for strikeouts."

Babe shows his early pitching form.

During the rest of the season, Babe pitched many more times. In most games he struck out at least twenty batters. "I threw the ball well," Babe said, "but Brother Matthias made me a pitcher. He knew baseball and loved it."

Jack Dunn, owner of the Baltimore Orioles, heard how well Babe pitched for St. Mary's. In February, 1914, he signed nineteen-year-old Babe to his first baseball contract.

"What do you think you're worth?" Jack Dunn asked Babe.

Babe's eyes opened wide in surprise. "You mean you'd pay me to play baseball?" Babe didn't realize people made money playing ball.

"I'll pay you $600 for the season," Jack Dunn said.

Babe laughed and signed the contract with his shaking left hand. At that time $600 was a lot of money.

On March 2, 1914, Babe left St. Mary's to start playing ball. Before saying good-bye, Brother Matthias shook Babe's hand and said, "You'll make it, George."

"Best of luck, George," shouted hundreds of St. Mary's boys as Babe walked out of the iron gates, wiping tears off his cheeks.

On the first day of spring training, Babe got his nickname. Jack Dunn was introducing his rookies to the veterans. "Look at Dunn and his newest babe," one of the old pros laughed. The name stayed with Babe for the rest of his life.

Babe was so excited with his new life that he got out of bed at dawn each day. Then he ran down to the train station to watch the trains go by. When he felt hungry, he ran back to the hotel and often ate twenty pancakes for breakfast.

After breakfast, Babe left the dining room to watch the hotel elevator. He had never seen an elevator before. One morning Babe gave the elevator worker five dollars. Then Babe jumped in and ran the elevator by himself.

On Babe's first payday, many of the old pros laughed at him. "As soon as I got my first paycheck," Babe said, "I bought a bicycle. A bicycle was what I had wanted and prayed for during most of my young life."

Babe pitched so well in the minor leagues that the Boston Red Sox bought his contract from the Orioles.

The old Red Sox players didn't like Babe at first. Because Babe was a pitcher, they didn't want him to take batting practice. Since Babe wanted to improve his hitting, he took batting practice anyway. "One day," Babe said, "I found that all my bats had been neatly sawed in two!"

As a rookie pitcher in 1914, Babe won two games and lost one. During the season, Babe received a note from Brother Matthias, which said,

"You're doing fine George, I'm proud of you."

In 1915, Babe pitched so well he won eighteen games and lost just six. His speed, control, and curve ball struck out 112 batters. Babe's ten doubles, one triple, and four home runs helped the Red Sox win many games that year. At that time, the best home run hitters only hit ten per year.

Babe quickly became a good hitter for the Red Sox.

That season Babe became known for his sense of humor. Once, a player complained to the manager that Babe seldom used his own toothbrush. Babe laughed and said, "That's all right, you can use my toothbrush anytime."

After some games, Babe stepped on his teammates' straw hats and nailed their shoes to the floor. Once, he chased a teammate through a train station with a wooden snake.

Since Babe stayed out late at night, many Red Sox players called him a "playboy." To live up to that name, Babe wore silk shirts and two-toned shoes. Babe's Panama hats always had colorful bands around them. When his teammates slept in $3 per night hotel rooms, Babe partied in very expensive rooms.

Although Babe often stayed up late at night, he still played baseball well. In 1916, he won twenty-three games and lost twelve, striking out 170 batters. As a hitter, he cracked out five doubles, three triples, and three home runs. In the World Series, Babe pitched fourteen innings to beat the Brooklyn Dodgers 2-1.

In 1917 umpires created many problems for Babe. In one game an umpire called one of Babe's pitches a ball. Of course, Babe thought it was a strike.

"Keep your eyes open long enough to see when a ball goes over the plate," Babe yelled.

"Shut up," the ump shouted, "or I'll throw you out of the game."

"Throw me out of this game and I'll punch you," Babe screamed.

"You're out of this game right now," the ump said.

Babe lost his temper and hit the umpire. As a penalty, Babe was fined $100.00 and couldn't play for ten days. Despite that, he won twenty-three games and lost thirteen that year.

CHAPTER 3

In the 1918 season, the Red Sox manager asked Babe to hit more. Babe answered by hitting eleven homers, which tied him for the home run title. Pitching, Babe won thirteen games and lost seven. In the World Series, Babe pitched against the Chicago Cubs and won two games, setting a record for scoreless innings.

Since Babe was hitting so many homers in 1919, the Red Sox manager told him to play the outfield so he could play every day. Babe's twenty-nine home runs set an American and major league record that year!

Babe's record surprised the Red Sox manager

because he often caught Babe sneaking into the hotel at six in the morning!

The New York Yankees bought Babe Ruth from the Boston Red Sox in 1920 for $100,000. Some players were surprised that Babe was earning $20,000 per year. At that time most baseball players only earned about $3,000 per year.

Babe earned every cent of his pay that year when he hit fifty-four homers. This time Babe's record surprised his roommate, Ping Bodie.

"Who are you rooming with?" sportswriters asked Ping.

"Babe Ruth's suitcase," Ping laughed. "Babe is always out partying."

In the 1921 season the Yankee manager wanted Babe to hit more home runs. "Don't eat, drink, and party so much," he said. That night Babe went to bed at nine, and ate and drank half of what he usually did.

The next day Babe didn't get any hits. Although he obeyed his manager for three nights, Babe didn't get any hits for three days.

On the fourth night Babe didn't go to bed at all and ate fourteen hamburgers. The next day he hit two home runs, one over the center field scoreboard!

That season Babe's fifty-nine home runs and .378 batting average helped the Yankees win their first pennant. Babe didn't play well in the World

Babe gets in some batting practice as a Yankee.

Series. The Yankees lost to the New York Giants. Instead of playing, Babe should have been in a hospital. He had a deep cut on his left arm and a sprained left wrist. He limped in the outfield because he had pulled muscles in his legs.

After the World Series, Babe got into a lot of trouble. He played some practice baseball games for money. That was against baseball's rules, so Babe was fined over $3,000 and couldn't play until May 20, 1922.

Since Babe had such a late start in 1922, he played poorly for the rest of the season. To make things worse, he ate and drank more than usual, and was out of shape. Before most games, Babe partied all night.

A typical Babe Ruth supper was a whole chicken and three pounds of potatoes. For dessert, he'd eat a quart of ice cream. Once, Babe even ate a whole custard pie. For midnight snacks, he ate six ham and cheese sandwiches and drank six bottles of pop.

Fans booed Babe when he played poorly that year. Once, Babe chased a booing fan around the grandstands. For that, he was fined $100.00 and couldn't play for many games.

After that season, Jimmy Walker, a New York state senator, scolded Babe for his poor behavior. "You have let down the kids of America," Walker said. "They think of you as their hero and look up to

Before the start of spring training each year, Babe usually played golf.

Lou Gehrig (right), another famous Yankee player, and Babe exchange batting tips during spring training.

you. But, you party and hurt your body."

Tears slid down Babe Ruth's cheeks.

"If I did not love you," Walker said, "I would not tell you these things. Will you promise, for the kids of America, to change your ways?"

Babe wiped tears from his eyes, "So help me, Jim, I will."

On April 18, 1923, 75,000 fans jammed into Yankee Stadium for opening day. It was the newest ball park in the country and many fans called it "the house that Ruth built." To give his fans something to cheer about, Babe hit a home run in the fourth inning.

Babe behaved and played well for the rest of the year. His forty-one home runs and .393 batting average helped the Yankees win the flag. In the World Series, Babe hit three home runs. He helped the Yankees win the title for the first time.

Superstition played an important part in Babe's baseball life. When he trotted in from the outfield, he always stepped on second base. He always left his hotel by a side door to go to the ball park. White butterflies were good luck in the outfield. Others Babe chased away with his glove.

Babe is shown here with his pet calf, Flossy, on his farm near Sudbury, Massachusettes in 1924.

CHAPTER 4

For Babe, 1924 was an even better year. He won the American League batting title with a .378 average and he knocked out forty-six home runs!

"I saw no reason why I couldn't party both day and night," Babe said in 1925. As a result, Babe had a poor season. He was older now, and eating and drinking too much really hurt his body. Babe's batting average dropped to .290. He hit only twenty-five home runs.

Babe was out of shape and stayed out all night. He was fined $5,000 and not allowed to play in many games. "I am not proud of this part of my baseball life," Babe said years later. "I wish I could change what I did. Those bad times taught me a lesson. I had acted like a spoiled child."

When Babe saw he was hurting the Yankees, he told them he was sorry. "I promise I will do better," he said.

After that poor season, Babe worked to get in shape in Artie McGovern's gym in New York City. "I boxed, played handball, and worked on exercise machines," Babe said. "Artie threw a medicine ball at my belly until I was red and sore! When I left for spring training, I was as hard as nails and in great shape."

All Babe's hard work paid off in the 1926 baseball season. He hit forty-seven home runs and his batting average was .372.

Miller Huggins, the great Yankee manager, told Babe, "I respect a man who can win over himself."

"That made me feel real good," Babe said.

Babe and his first wife relax at their Sudbury farm. Mrs. Ruth was later killed in a fire.

George Sisler (right), the great player for the St. Louis Browns, greets Babe. The Cardinals beat the Yankees in the 1926 World Series.

One day in 1926, a doctor telephoned Babe Ruth. He told Babe about a boy named Johnny Sylvester who had just had surgery and was dying. "I think you could help the boy get well if you saw him," the doctor said.

Before the game that afternoon, Babe visited Johnny. Babe talked with him about home runs and the Yankees, and signed a baseball for him.

"Babe," Johnny said, before Babe left for the game, "hit one for me today, please."

"Sure, kid," Babe smiled.

That day Babe Ruth hit a home run for Johnny Sylvester.

After the game, the doctor telephoned Babe again. "We noticed a change in Johnny right after you hit the homer," he said. "He had lost his will to live. You gave it back to him."

Johnny Sylvester was just one of the thousands of children Babe visited in hospitals. Although Babe himself was afraid of hospitals, he visited them often. The sick children hugged and kissed Babe, and climbed all over him. Many of them had refused to move for doctors.

After talking with the young people, Babe gave them some good advice. "No boy who wants to be a big leaguer should smoke," he said.

When he left the hospital, parents, doctors, and nurses always thanked Babe for helping the children.

Sick children made Babe feel unhappy. His wife said that Babe sat alone in the kitchen many nights and cried for the children who hurt so much.

Babe loved children and did all he could for them. One evening, after a double-header in Yankee Stadium, Babe was driving home. When he stopped near a park for a red light, his car was surrounded by boys.

"Come on, Babe," they yelled, "let's see you hit a few."

Although tired and dressed in a silk shirt, Babe smiled and got out of his car. For the next half hour, he hit ball after ball to the thrilled youngsters.

Once, Babe invited seven hundred orphans to a baseball game. He bought each one a bag of peanuts and a hat. Before the game, Babe even played music with the orphanage band.

In 1927, Babe Ruth hit his record setting sixty home runs. To do that, he had to play many games with pain. In one game Babe dislocated a finger while swinging at a pitch. Instead of quitting, Babe stayed in the game. He just asked the catcher to pull the finger back in place. When Babe swung and missed the next pitch, the finger popped out again. The catcher pulled it back in again. On the next pitch, Babe hit a home run!

During September, 1927, Babe hit seventeen home runs! That was more than one home run every two games! On the last day of the season, Babe hit his sixtieth. "I knew I was going to hit it," he laughed.

Sportswriters asked Babe how he hit so many home runs. "I swing as hard as I can," he said. "When the pitch comes speeding in, I try to swing right through the ball. I swing at that little ball with everything I've got in my body. I hit big or miss big!"

Another reason Babe hit so many home runs was that his timing was perfect. His wrists snapped

Babe watches his sixtieth home run of the 1927 season go over the fence. This record stood until 1961, when Roger Maris hit sixty-one homers.

Babe enjoyed hunting. Here he is shown on a pheasant hunt in the state of New York.

the bat into the ball at just the right second.

After the 1927 season, sportswriters voted Babe "Player of the Year." They didn't give him the prize for his sixty home runs. "They honored me because of the comeback I made after my poor

1925 season," Babe said. "At that time many writers had said that I was all washed up."

CHAPTER 5

The 1928 baseball season was another great one for Babe Ruth. He blasted fifty-four home runs and helped the Yankees win the pennant again.

No one has ever played a better World Series than Babe did that year. He had ten hits in sixteen at bats and scored nine runs. His batting average was .625! For the second time, Babe hit three home runs in one World Series game!

To relax in the off-season, Babe went fishing and hunting. Often, he cleaned and cooked his day's catch. Babe made tasty barbecue and spaghetti sauces. After dinner, he sang and played cards.

Babe's legs began hurting him during the 1929 season. Ignoring the pain, he hit forty-six home runs.

Near the end of that season, Miller Huggins, the Yankee manager, died. Babe knew his own playing days were almost over and wanted to be a manager. "I've been around the majors for sixteen years," Babe told the Yankees' owner, "and with the Yankees for ten years. I know baseball inside and

Babe (second from right) and some friends show their day's catch.

Babe married Claire Hodgson in April 1929. It was his second marriage.

out. Because of my pitching career, I know the game more than most people. I know how to handle pitchers because I was one. I know how to handle batters because I was one. I want to manage the Yankees."

"You party around too much, Babe," the Yankee owner said. "Since you can't manage yourself, how can you manage the Yankees?"

"If I don't know how to manage myself," Babe replied, "I wouldn't be in baseball today."

The owner listened to Babe, but did not hire him to manage the team. Babe felt unhappy and told sportswriters the Yankees weren't treating him fairly.

Although thirty-five years old in 1930, Babe played better than most rookies. That season he knocked out forty-nine home runs and had a .359 batting average.

Managing the Yankees was still one of Babe's goals. He was mature enough now and wasn't a playboy anymore. The Yankees owner hurt Babe again when he hired another manager.

Babe never held a grudge against anyone. Although upset, he played well for the Yankees in 1931. He hit .373 and smashed forty-six home runs over the fences.

Many young people wanted to grow up to be like Babe Ruth. Whenever he could, Babe told them the life of a ball player wasn't easy. "I can't go to the movies because I might hurt my eyes. I can't dance because they tell me it's bad for my legs. I can't go to a nightclub because they'd say I was drinking. I can't read a book on a train because it's too hard on my eyes. I can't travel on airplanes because it's against the rules of my contract and my insurance. I can't enjoy golf because people always follow me for autographs."

Babe spent much of his free time listening to the radio shows. THE LONE RANGER, THE GREEN

Babe surprised everyone when he safely stole home in a 1932 game against the St. Louis Browns.

HORNET, GANGBUSTERS, and THE FBI IN PEACE AND WAR were some of his favorites.

1932 was a good year for the aging Babe. He hit forty-one home runs and had a .341 batting average. That fall Babe played in his tenth World

Babe was a proud father. He is shown here with Dorothy (left), a daughter from his first marriage, and Julia, Claire's daughter from a previous marriage.

Series. In the third game against the Cubs, he hit his most famous home run.

It was in the fourth inning at Wrigley Field in Chicago when Babe stepped into the batter's box. Cub fans wanted to upset Babe, so they threw tomatoes and lemons at him.

"Hey, balloon head," some Cub players shouted at Babe, "don't let your belly get in the way of your bat!"

Babe just smiled confidently and tipped his cap.

"Just before the first pitch," Babe told sportswriters later, "I pointed to deep center field." Babe was telling Cub fans and players where he was going to hit a home run. "Then the pitcher threw one right across the plate and I let it go. But, before the umpire could call it a strike, which it was, I raised my right hand. I stuck out one finger and yelled, 'Strike one!'"

When the Cub fans and players saw that, they razzed Babe more than before.

"The pitcher threw another one right across the plate," Babe said. "Again, I stepped back, held up my right hand and yelled, 'Strike two!'"

Before the next pitch, Babe stepped out of the batter's box and pointed to center field again.

Cub fans and players knew Babe was razzing them, so they threw more things at Babe and called him more names.

Babe just smiled and tipped his cap again.

"Then the pitcher threw me a fast ball," Babe said. "I swung with everything I had. As I hit the ball, every muscle, every sense I had told me I had never hit a better one. I knew that as long as I lived nothing would ever feel as good as that. I didn't have to look, but I did. That ball just went on and on. It hit far up in the center field bleachers in the spot I had pointed to.

"It was the proudest moment I had ever had in baseball."

In 1933, fans could see that the great Babe Ruth was slowing down. "The old legs were getting tired," Babe said. As a result, his batting average dropped to .301 and he only hit thirty-four home runs.

CHAPTER 6

1934 was Babe's last year with the New York Yankees. Many fans cried when they saw Babe strike out and miss fly balls in the outfield. "It was becoming hard for me to move my legs," Babe said. "My batting average dropped to .288 and I only hit twenty-two home runs."

Babe Ruth was traded to the Boston Braves

The Ruth family celebrated Babe's fortieth birthday in 1935.

before the 1935 season. Although Babe tried to play well for the fans, his body just couldn't perform as it had.

"The harder I tried," Babe said, "the worse I did. It was hard for me even to run down to first base. I was forty-one and playing my twenty-second season in the big leagues. Rookies were striking me out or making me pop up on balls I could have hit out of the lot a few years before. It was a rotten feeling."

May 30, 1935, was the last day Babe played.

Managing interested Babe even more after he quit playing, "I wanted to stay in baseball," Babe said, "more than I ever wanted anything in my life."

No owners hired Babe to manage their teams. "I felt really lost without baseball," Babe said. "I went to a lot of games at Yankee Stadium. But I just didn't feel right sitting in the stands. I had to do something active so I turned to golf and played every hour possible. Without golf, I would have gone nuts."

Three years later, in 1938, Babe got a coaching job with the Brooklyn Dodgers. He coached well for a while, but didn't feel well, so he quit.

After that season, Babe spent most of his time golfing and visiting hospitals and orphanages.

In 1946, a sharp pain began hurting Babe's face and jaw. "My left eye closed," Babe said, "and I couldn't eat and seldom could speak."

Babe had surgery, but didn't feel well until the children of America wrote to him. Thirty thousand boys and girls sent Babe get well cards and notes. "I know this will be your sixty-first home run," one young person wrote Babe. "You will hit it."

Babe returned to Yankee Stadium eight weeks before he died. In a special ceremony, Uniform No. 3 was retired — no Yankee would ever wear that number again.

Although Babe felt better for a while, the pain grew worse.

On August 16, 1948, Babe Ruth died from cancer. Thousands of people miss him and will never forget what a great ballplayer he was.

In 1949, a plaque in memory of Babe was placed in Yankee Stadium. Mrs. Ruth is pictured with Mayor O'Dwyer (left) and Governor Dewey. The plaque at the left honors Miller Huggins, Yankee manager during Babe's best years.

46

IF YOU ENJOYED THIS STORY, THERE ARE MORE LEGENDS TO READ ABOUT:

PELÉ! THE SPORTS CAREER OF EDSON DO NASCIMENTO

HENRY! THE SPORTS CAREER OF HENRY AARON

TARK! THE SPORTS CAREER OF FRANCIS TARKENTON

BROWN! THE SPORTS CAREER OF JAMES BROWN

PATTY! THE SPORTS CAREER OF PATRICIA BERG

THORPE! THE SPORTS CAREER OF JAMES THORPE

ZAHARIAS! THE SPORTS CAREER OF MILDRED ZAHARIAS

SAYERS! THE SPORTS CAREER OF GALE SAYERS

CASEY! THE SPORTS CAREER OF CHARLES STENGEL

KILLY! THE SPORTS CAREER OF JEAN-CLAUDE KILLY

CHRIS! THE SPORTS CAREER OF CHRIS EVERT LLOYD

BABE! THE SPORTS CAREER OF GEORGE RUTH

KING! THE SPORTS CAREER OF BILLIE JEAN KING

WILT! THE SPORTS CAREER OF WILTON CHAMBERLAIN

ALI! THE SPORTS CAREER OF MUHAMMAD ALI